Veterans Day

Mir Tamim Ansary

Heinemann Library
Chicago, Illinois

© 1999, 2006 Heinemann Library
a division of Reed Elsevier Inc.
Chicago, Illinois

Customer Service 888-454-2279
Visit our website at www.heinemannraintree.com

All rights reserved. No part of this publication may be reproduced or transmitted in any form or by any means, electronic or mechanical, including photocopying, recording, taping, or any information storage and retrieval system, without permission in writing from the publisher.

Designed by Kimberly Miracle and Q2A Creative
Printed in China by South China Printing Company

12 11 10
10 9 8 7 6 5

New edition ISBNs: 1-4034-8893-2 (hardcover)   978-1-4034-8893-0(hardcover)
                          1-4034-8906-8 (paperback)   978-1-4034-8906-7(paperback)

The Library of Congress has cataloged the first edition as follows:
Ansary, Mir Tamim.
        Veterans Day / Mir Tamim Ansary.
            p. cm. -- (Holiday histories)
        Includes bibliographical references and index.
        Summary: Introduces Veterans Day, explaining the historical events behind it, how it became a holiday, and how it is observed.
        ISBN 1-57572-876-1 (lib. bdg.)
        1. Veterans Day – Juvenile literature. [1. Veterans Day. 2. Holidays.] I. Title. II. Series: Ansary, Mir Tamim. Holiday histories.

D671 .A75 1998
394.264 – dc21
                                        9814376

Acknowledgments
The author and publishers are grateful to the following for permission to reproduce photographs: AP/Wide World pp. 6, 7, 13 (all), 16, 18 (right), 19, 22, 26 (right), 28; Corbis pp. 12, 24-25 (Wally McNamee); Corbis-Bettmann pp. 8 (Alexander Alland Sr.), 18 (left), 20 (Baldwin H. Ward), 23; The Granger Collection pp. 9, 18 (center); Stock Boston p. 4 (Bob Daemmrick); UPI/Corbis-Bettmann pp. 10, 11, 14; SuperStock pp. 15 (all), 26 (left); Reuters/Corbis-Bettmann p. 27.

Cover photograph reproduced with permission of Alex Segre/Alamy.

Every effort has been made to contact copyright holders of any material reproduced in this book. Any omissions will be rectified in subsequent printings if notice is given to the publisher.

Disclaimer
All the Internet addresses (URLs) given in this book were valid at the time of going to press. However, due to the dynamic nature of the Internet, some addresses may have changed, or sites may have changed or ceased to exist since publication. While the author and publisher regret any inconvenience this may cause readers, no responsibility for any such changes can be accepted by either the author or the publisher.

Contents

Some words are shown in bold, **like this**. You can find out what they mean by looking in the glossary.

A Day for Veterans

November 11 is Veterans Day in the United States. A crowd has gathered in the park to watch a parade.

Many people think this is just another day off from school or work. But Veterans Day means much more to these people. That is because they are veterans themselves.

What Is a Veteran?

A veteran is someone who has been in the **armed forces**. Many of these veterans fought in wars. Some fought in the Persian Gulf War in 1991.

Some even fought in World War Two, way back in the 1940s. All these veterans risked their lives for our country.

Before Veterans Day

How did this holiday begin? Let's go back to a time before Veterans Day. Your great grandparents were young then. The United States was at peace.

But **Europe** was **tense**. In Europe, many small countries were ruled by bigger ones. Millions of angry people wanted to be free.

World War!

Some of the big countries wanted more land.
Their neighbors in other countries did as well.
Both sides were building strong armies.

In 1914 a war began. Germany helped one side. Russia helped the other. Soon more than sixteen countries were fighting.

The United States Fights

German submarines started sinking U.S. ships.
The United States decided to fight Germany.
In 1917 U.S. **troops** sailed to **Europe**.

The fighting stopped on November 11 at 11 o'clock, when Germany **surrendered**. World War One was over. More than fourteen million people had died.

Armistice Day

In 1919 President Woodrow Wilson called November 11 a holiday. He called it Armistice Day. Armistice means "to stop fighting."

That day many people wore red poppies. They
did so to remember Flanders Field. A bloody
battle was fought in that poppy field.

Honoring Peace

At eleven o'clock that day, many people became quiet. They kept silent for two minutes. This was a way to **honor** the peace.

These **customs** were repeated every year after that. People gave thanks for peace. They honored the soldiers who had won the peace.

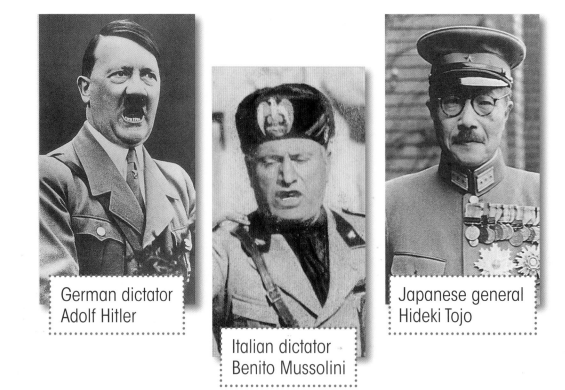

German dictator
Adolf Hitler

Italian dictator
Benito Mussolini

Japanese general
Hideki Tojo

Trouble Again

But the peace did not last. Cruel **dictators** took
over Germany and Italy. Powerful generals took
over Japan.

These countries were called the Axis Powers.
In 1935 they started to attack other countries.
They planned to take over the world.

World War Two

The world fought back. In 1939 World War Two
began. It was much more deadly than World War
One. Armies now had more powerful guns.

The war spread all over the world. There was
fighting in more than 50 countries. There were
battles on land, at sea, and in the air.

The Axis Powers Fail

In 1941 Japanese airplanes bombed U.S. ships and planes in Hawaii. After that, the United States entered the war.

The Axis Powers were **defeated** in 1945. World War Two ended. More than 50 million people had died in this war.

Celebrating Veterans Today

After the war, Americans were glad to celebrate Armistice Day again. In 1954 the name Armistice Day was changed to Veterans Day.

Now on Veterans Day, we celebrate all our veterans. Most of all, we **honor** those who died. We thank them for all that we have. They gave all they had.

Our Armed Forces

Today we have a powerful army, air force, and navy. We have the Marines and the Coast Guard.

We stay ready even when there is no war. Our forces help keep peace in troubled places. We hope they can stop another war from starting.

The Eleventh Hour

The parade is over and the crowds are gone. But one veteran stays. This man loves peace because he has seen war. That is why he stands here on the eleventh day of the eleventh month.

The eleventh hour strikes at last. The veteran bows his head and falls silent. In his silence, he remembers friends who never came back from battle.

Important Dates

Veterans Day

1914	World War One begins
1914	The Battle of Flanders Field
1917	The United States enters the war
1918	World War One ends
1919	Armistice Day becomes a national holiday
1922	Mussolini takes power in Italy
1926	Army officers take power in Japan
1933	Hitler takes power in Germany
1939	World War Two begins
1941	Japan bombs U.S. ships at Pearl Harbor, in Hawaii
1945	World War Two ends
1954	Armistice Day is changed to Veterans Day

Glossary

armed forces   country's army, air force, and navy

customs   things people always do on special days or for certain events

defeated   beaten

dictators   leaders who use force to govern

Europe   one of the seven continents

honor   show respect for something

surrendered   gave up

tense   full of worry

troops   soldiers

Find Out More

Landau, Elaine. *Veterans Day: Remembering Our War Heroes.*
    Berkeley Heights, NJ: Enslow, 2002.
Schaefer, Ted and Lola Schaefer. *The Vietnam Veterans Memorial.*
    Chicago: Heinemann Library, 2006.
Schuh, Mari C. *Veterans Day.* Mankato, Minn.: Capstone, 2003.

The Department of Veterans Affairs - Kids Page
http://www.va.gov/Kids/k-5/index.asp

Index